MW00940546

A Complete Guide to Written Accent Marks in Spanish

With exercises

Third Edition

By
Tom Mathews, Ph.D.
Professor of Spanish
Weber State University

ORGLE PRESS
San Francisco

First edition:	1996
	1998-published online
	2001-included information for making marks on a computer
Second edition:	2010-updated to include changes made by the Academia Real
Third edition:	2013-includes exercises

Table of Contents

Foreword

My webpage on the use of accent marks in Spanish has for years been at or near the top of any "Google" search on the topic and I'm pleased that my explanation has been of use to teachers and students. Recently, I have received several requests for a version in print and I have sensed a need for some limited practice exercises.

The intention of this explanation of accent marks is to be something between a brief introduction and an exhaustive compendium.

There are a number of short lessons on accent marks on the internet and most every Spanish textbook has a few pages on the topic at the end of an early chapter, but by and large none of these include enough detail or examples to make expert users of students. At the opposite extreme, the most recent *Ortografía de la lengua española* (2010) published by the Real Academia devotes a full 87 pages of small print to the subject.

My goal here is to be thorough but not overwhelming or pedantic. I aim to provide an explanation that is appropriate for students of Spanish with limited background in linguistics and to provide exercises of progressive difficulty so that these same students can become adept, if not expert, at using accent marks in their writing.

Preliminaries

Definitions and the basic rules

1

Why accent marks?

In Spanish, the **acute accent mark**, sloping downward from right to left (✔), is used to identify stressed vowels. Yet most stressed vowels in Spanish do not need an accent mark: a simple pair of basic rules tells us which vowel (or syllable) to stress in the vast majority of words. The written accent mark exists to identify exceptions, where simply following the basic rules would result in mispronunciation. These rules are presented in the next section.

Other diacritical marks in Spanish
Of course, Spanish uses the **tilde** (∼) over the letter 'n' to represent a palatalized nasal.

Spanish also uses the **diaeresis** (in Spanish, *diéresis* or *crema*): this is made of two small dots placed horizontally over a vowel (▪▪). The diaeresis is used, over the letter 'u' in Spanish, in the sequence 'gue' or 'gui' to indicate that the vowel needs to be pronounced. Compare the following:

guerra ['ge-ra] **güera** ['gwe-ra]
guisar [gi-'sar] **lingüística** [liŋ-'guis-ti-ka]

There are several marks commonly used in other languages, but never in Spanish. Among these:

Grave accent mark	à	Circumflex accent	ô
Breve	ĕ	Macron	ū
Carat or háček	ǐ	Cedilla	ç

2

The basic rules

These are the two basic rules for the use of written accent marks in Spanish. They will account for the vast majority of accent marks. The purpose of this little book is to show how and why these rules work and to explain the few exceptions.

1. If a word ends in a vowel, or 'n' or 's', the stress is normally on the next to the last syllable.

2. If a word ends in a consonant other than 'n' or 's', the stress is normally on the last syllable.

HOWEVER: If the stress in a word doesn't follow rules 1 and 2, then the syllable that is stressed needs a written accent mark over the vowel.

The rules and explanations presented throughout this book reflect the changes made by the twenty-two national *Academias de la Lengua Española* in Guadalajara, Mexico, on November 28, 2010.

3

On the relationship between spelling and pronunciation

It's worth pointing out that written systems, particularly alphabetical systems, reflect spoken language. Speaking came first; only later did humans invent writing systems as a way to record their language. In Spanish, this means that a written accent mark exists to let a reader know how well-educated speakers of the language pronounce the word.

If you are reading a text and come across a word that you don't know or have never heard before, the Spanish spelling system is precise enough that you will be able to pronounce it perfectly. True, you'll likely not know what it means, but you'll pronounce it well.

This is generally not true in English. Often, if a student comes across an unknown word in an English text, he or she will need to look the word up or ask someone how it's pronounced. English language dictionaries usually indicate pronunciation after each entry, something completely unnecessary in Spanish.

Now, what happens in Spanish if a word is misspelled? Universally there is mispronunciation or confusion. In the **Exercises** in Part 2, I have included isolated words and words in context that are purposely written incorrectly; that is, without an accent mark. In each case, you will be expected to supply the mark. This works well if you know the words in question, but if you don't, how will you know where to put the accent mark? I suggest that you ask a fluent or native speaker to read the words or passages to you so you can hear where the stresses fall and then make an educated decision as to where an accent mark might be needed.

Part One

Stress and pronunciation in Spanish

1

The syllable in Spanish

A **syllable**, in Spanish or English, is a single vowel sound
surrounded by other sounds that may naturally group with it.
Many syllables are made up of just one vowel and nothing else.
Here are some examples marked in boxes. All of the syllables
are separated with hyphens.

| a |- no – che | o |- jo | y |
| e |- sos | o | | u |- nas

A syllable may contain other sounds that group with the vowel.
These sounds are most commonly **consonants** but may also
be **glides**. A glide is written as a vowel but pronounced with
some sort of friction or closure of the lips. In Spanish, the
letters 'i' and 'u', if found next to another vowel, are usually
pronounced as a glide and form one syllable with the vowel
they accompany.

| tie |- ne | bue |- no   ha - | cien |- da
| cual | na - | ción | | siem |- pre

In these examples the written vowel 'i' is pronounced as [j] or
like the 'y' in *yellow*. The 'u' when part of a diphthong is
pronounced as [w] as is *quick* or *swan*.

There are two kinds of syllables in Spanish: those that are
stressed (*tónicas*) and those that are unstressed (*átonas*).
One-syllable words will be either **tónicas** or **átonas**.

In words of more than one syllable, only one will be stressed.[1]

Stressed vs unstressed syllables
In the following paragraph all of the stressed syllables are shown in boxes.

Aquí todo va de mal en peor. La semana pasada se murió mi tía Jacinta, y el sábado, cuando ya la habíamos enterrado y comenzaba a bajársenos la tristeza, comenzó a llover como nunca. A mi papá eso le dio coraje, porque toda la cosecha de cebada estaba asoleándose en el solar. Y el aguacero llegó de repente, en grandes olas de agua, sin darnos tiempo ni siquiera a esconder aunque fuera un manojo.[2]

Notice that sometimes the stressed syllables have an accent mark, but that usually they don't. Notice also that an unstressed syllable will never, ever, have an accent mark. Let's read that again: AN UNSTRESSED SYLLABLE WILL NEVER HAVE AN ACCENT MARK! Some one-syllable words are stressed and some are not. If you want to write a word and you don't know

---

[1] English allows secondary stresses within a word; generally, Spanish does not.
[2] Rulfo, J. (1969). "Es que somos muy pobres" *El llano en llamas*. México, D.F.: Fondo de Cultura Económica. p. 28.

which syllable is stressed and which ones aren't, try pronouncing the word out loud, or ask a native speaker to pronounce it for you, or look it up in a good dictionary.

Part 1: 1.1 Counting syllables[3]

Count the number of syllables in each word and then enter the number in the blank space.

1. ___ mesa
2. ___ lento
3. ___ fatalidad
4. ___ triste
5. ___ lastimosamente
6. ___ contento
7. ___ mostrador
8. ___ adulterado
9. ___ falta
10. ___ pontífice
11. ___ hipotético
12. ___ contabilidad

Part 1: 1.2 Stressed syllables

In each word, circle the stressed vowel or syllable.

1. humorosa
2. juegan
3. síntomas
4. cantad
5. restaurante
6. sábana
7. frijol
8. frijoles
9. árboles
10. asistente
11. mostrador
12. ligeramente

---

[3] Counting syllables is most easily done by tapping your fingers on a tabletop, as if you were playing the piano.

2

Diphthongs in Spanish

The vowels *a*, *e*, and *o* are strong in Spanish. They always form their own syllable wherever they appear. The vowels *u* and *i* are weak, and only form their own syllable when they are separate from other vowels. When a weak vowel is next to a strong vowel or another weak vowel, they **automatically** form a diphthong, that is, just one syllable. And their pronunciation weakens into [j] or [w] as explained earlier. These glides can never have an accent mark written above them.

Diphthongs

In the following examples the number of syllables in each word is shown in parentheses after the word. The stressed syllables are in boldface.

Strong vowels (*a*, *e*, *o*) always form their own syllables:

o - tor - **gar** (3)	**ra** - na (2)
a - van - **za** - da (4)	**co** - rre - o (3)
Es - **pa** - ña (3)	ha - **blar** (2)
a - po - **sen** - to (4)	**sá** - ba - na (3)

Weak vowels (*i*, *u*) form their own syllable if they are "surrounded" by consonants:

tri - bu (2)	**mi** - to (2)
ci - ne (2)	**mís** - ti - co (3)

cu - bo (2)

la - rin - **gi** - tis (4)

fút - bol (2)

es - **pí** - ri - tu (4)

Otherwise, weak vowels form a diphthong with the strong vowel that is next to them:

lue - go (2)

a - **diós** (2)

buey (1)

dio (1)

tie - nes (2)

co - **mió** (2)

far - ma - **céu** - ti - co (5)

que - **réis** (2)

El hiato

In any word where two strong vowels occur together (with no intervening consonant) they are counted and pronounced as separate syllables. The resulting lengthening or break is called **hiato** (from the Latin *'hiatus'* meaning 'break'). Whenever two vowels do not form a diphthong together (one of them being pronounced a [j] or [w]) we say "*las vocales están en hiato*".

le - **ó** - nes (3)

cre - o (2)

be - **a** - tos (3)

rí - o (2)

a - ta - **úd** (3)

sa - **bí** - a (3)

Part 1: 2.1 Finding Diphthongs

In the following words, circle each diphthong. Remember that only 'i' and 'u' from diphthongs; the strong vowels are in hiato and are pronounced as separate syllables.

1. generación
2. muestra
3. maestra
4. hiato
5. cazuela
6. teatral
7. espontáneo
8. licuefacción
9. aéreo
10. concupiscencia
11. saeta
12. europeo

Part 1: 2.2 Finding 'hitao'

This is the same list of words, but now, circle each example of hitao.

1. generación
2. muestra
3. maestra
4. hiato
5. cazuela
6. teatral
7. espontáneo
8. licuefacción
9. aéreo
10. concupiscencia
11. saeta
12. europeo

Part 1: 2.3 Counting syllables

Finally, count the number of syllables in each word and then enter the number in the blank space.

1. ___ generación
2. ___ muestra
3. ___ maestra
4. ___ hiato
5. ___ cazuela
6. ___ teatral

7. ___ espontáneo
8. ___ licuefacción
9. ___ aéreo
10. ___ concupiscencia
11. ___ saeta
12. ___ europeo

3

One-syllable words

One-syllable words in Spanish never carry an accent mark unless they fall into the group described in Part Two, Section 2. Don't get in the habit of putting accent marks on one-syllable words as some sort of ornament. Don't put an accent mark on a one-syllable word unless you know why!

The current rule was adopted in 1959 by the *Real Academia Española*.[4] There are still many native speakers (most of them either old and educated before the new rules or not well educated at all) who continue to put accent marks on many one-syllable words (particularly verbs). Don't do it! It's a nasty habit.

---

[4] Real Academia Española (1959). *Nuevas normas de prosodia y ortografía*. Madrid.

Part 1: 3.1 Counting syllables in one-syllable words

Yes. OK. This is silly. But pay attention to the diphthongs and don't be fooled. These are all one syllable words.

1. ___ las
2. ___ pues
3. ___ diez
4. ___ guion
5. ___ aun
6. ___ buen

7. ___ ya
8. ___ buey
9. ___ fui
10. ___ dios
11. ___ vio
12. ___ cien

Part 1: 3.2 Pronouncing words written wrong

Putting an accent mark on a strong vowel in these words does nothing but make you look inadequate. Putting an accent mark on a vowel that should form a diphthong makes a strange two syllable word. Try to pronounce these words as written.

1. pues/*púes (POOH-es)
2. diez/*díez (DEE-es)
3. guion/*guíon (GEE-ohn)
4. aun/aún (this is a word!)
5. buen/*búen (BOO-en)

7. buey/*búey (BOO-ey)
8. fui/*fuí (no change, still *fui*)
9. dios/*díos (DEE-ohs)
10. vio/*vío (VEE-oh)
11. cien/*cíen (SEE-en)

4

Polysyllabic words

There are four categories of multisyllabic words in Spanish, as far as stress is concerned. A word's stress category has to do with which syllable is *tónica*.

- Palabras **llanas** are stressed on the next to the last syllable (*la penúltima*).

- Palabras **agudas** are stressed on the last syllable (*la última*).

- Palabras **esdrújulas** are stressed on the third to the last syllable (*la antepenúltima*).

- Palabras **sobresdrújulas** are stressed on the fourth to the last syllable.

Palabras llanas
All of the following words are stressed on the next to last syllable (*o la penúltima sílaba*).

no - che	**ár** - bol
bi - **go** - te	**pe** - rro
ca - **ba** - llo	co - **ci** - na
fa - bu - **lo** - so	**lib** - ro
ac - ci - **den** - te	fi - lo - so - **fí** - a
es - ta - **cio** - nes	**hi** - jos
cés - ped	sa - **ra** – pe

Palabras agudas

Each of the following words is stressed on the last syllable (*o la última sílaba*).

fri - **jol**

hab - **ló**

so - por - **tar**

ma - ra - **tón**

ñan - **dú**

sar - **tén**

can - **tar**

an - **dén**

sen - **tí**

re - **loj**

baj - **ó**

pin - **cel**

Palabras esdrújulas

All of the following words are stressed on the third to the last syllable (*o la antepenúltima sílaba*). Notice that esdrújulas always have a written accent mark.

fan - **tás** - ti - co

én - fa - sis

lu - **ciér** - na - ga

es - **drú** - ju - la

ri - **dí** - cu - lo

sín - te - sis

pa - ra - **lí** - ti - co

es - **tú** - pi - dos

mur - **cié** - la - go

miér - co - les

an - **gé** - li - cas

a - **ná** - li - sis

Palabras sobresdrújulas

I'll go out on a limb and say that no "real" words in Spanish are stressed on anything but one of the last three syllables. However, many "unreal" words are stressed on the fourth to the last syllable or even earlier (*una sílaba preantepenúltima*). Most dictionaries and grammar texts do in fact define these preantepentults as words.

All of them fall into two categories:

(1) verbs in the gerund or command forms with two enclitic pronouns, and
(2) adjectives with antepenultimate stress that have been converted into adverbs with the addition of *-mente*.

In both cases these are written in modern Spanish as one word, but syntactically and rhythmically they are interpreted as either compound words or separate words. In any case, they will always carry an accent mark.

Verbs with two pronouns
The following examples are either a verb conjugated as a gerund (*-ando*, *-iendo*) to which two pronouns or unstressed clitics have been attached, or a command with two pronouns.[5]

fu - **mán** - do - me - la
es - cri - **bién** - do - se - lo
di - **cién** - do - te – lo
trá - e - me - los

---

[5] If these same pronouns are used before the verb, they are written separately:
  (a) *Me encantan estos zapatos. Paco está comprándomelos.*
     or *Paco me los está comprando.*
  (b) *Quiero escuchar el chiste. ¡Cuéntamelo!*
     or *¡No me lo cuentes!*

cóm - pra - me - las
lím - pia - te - los

Adverbs with -mente

Almost any adjective (in the feminine singular form) can be converted into an adverb with the addition of the word 'mente'. You're probably thinking that 'mente' is a suffix while I have called it a word. Well, two things argue for it being a word even though it is written as part of the adjective it's working with. First, the word 'mente' in Spanish is feminine and singular, as in '*Mi abuela tiene la mente sana*'. This explains the need for a feminine, singular adjective to go with it. Here are a few examples:

profundamente
altamente
extensamente

Second, if we wish to use several such adverbs in the same phrase, we use the word 'mente' only once, after the last adjective. Again, a couple of examples:

En clase contesté lenta y estúpidamente.
Mi padre es un gigante tanto mental y espiritual
como emocionalmente.

So then, when we add 'mente' to an adjective the result is a pseudo-word with two stresses: one on the adjective half and one on the 'mente'. In practice, this merely means that all of these adverbs must be pronounced as if they were two words. These are the only words in Spanish that have secondary stress (a phenomenon that is quite common in English). As for accent marks, if the adjective takes an accent mark by itself, it keeps it when combined with 'mente'.

rápidamente
fácilmente
hipotéticamente
fantásticamente
económicamente
físicamente

But

tristemente
lentamente
felizmente
absolutamente

The next few examples have to do with pronunciation and are generally unrelated to accent marks. Still, this is fascinating stuff.

English has a general distaste for stress clashes; that is, if the last syllable in an English word normally would be stressed and the first syllable in the next word is stressed, speakers will shift one stress or the other so that the two stresses are separated by at least one syllable. Consider this example:

thir**teen**
thir**teen don**keys

When spoken in isolation the word 'thirteen' is stressed on the last syllable. (*How old are you? --Thirteen*). But, when followed by a stressed syllable, the stress in 'thirteen' shifts back to the first syllable, thus avoiding a clash. (*What did you buy at the fair today? --Thirteen donkeys*).

On the other hand, Spanish speakers rather relish a stress class. Any adjective that is aguda when combined with 'mente' creates such a clash and care must be taken by English speaking natives to avoid shifting the stress. Therefore, since the word 'espiritual' is aguda (stressed on the last syllable) and 'mente' is llana (stressed on its first syllable) we have a clash. We must pronounce it *es-pi-ri-**tual**-**men**-te* and avoid the temptation to move the stress and say **es-**pi**-ri-tual-**men**-te*.

Here are some examples:

fatalmente   musicalmente
literalmente   fenomenalmente
idealmente   fiscalmente

Part 1: 4.1 Which syllable is stressed?
All of the following words are written correctly with accent
marks where they belong. The stressed syllables are in
boldface. Identify each word as llana, aguda, esdrújula or
sobresdrújula.

	LLANA	AGUDA	ESDRÚJULA	SOBRES.
1. **pa**tio	❑	❑	❑	❑
2. na**riz**	❑	❑	❑	❑
3. sim**pá**tico	❑	❑	❑	❑
4. **sá**bana	❑	❑	❑	❑
5. contes**tó**	❑	❑	❑	❑
6. con**tes**to	❑	❑	❑	❑
7. ac**ción**	❑	❑	❑	❑
8. ac**cio**nes	❑	❑	❑	❑
9. mur**cié**lago	❑	❑	❑	❑
10. hi**pér**baton	❑	❑	❑	❑
11. ca**du**co	❑	❑	❑	❑
12. frene**sí**	❑	❑	❑	❑
13. man**dí**bula	❑	❑	❑	❑
14. intere**san**te	❑	❑	❑	❑
15. **quí**tamelo	❑	❑	❑	❑

Part 1: 4.2 Pronunciation practice

Carefully exaggerating the stressed syllables, pronounce out loud the following sets of related words. Can you tell the difference in meaning that results when you change the stress?

1. **can**to   can**tó**
2. **hab**le   hab**lé**
3. **sá**bana   sa**ba**na
4. con**ti**nuo   conti**nú**o
5. ac**tuó**   ac**tú**o
6. **ha**cia   ha**cí**a
7. **rí**o   **ri**o
8. Ma**rí**a   **Ma**rio
9. **vín**culo   vincu**ló**
10. **aun**   a**ún**
11. **fin**es   fi**nés**
12. pa**pá**   **pa**pa
13. ma**má**   **ma**ma
14. mag**ní**fico   magni**fi**co   magnifi**có**
15. **cé**lebre   ce**le**bre   cele**bré**
16. **cán**tara   can**ta**ra   canta**rá**
17. **pú**blico   pu**bli**co   publi**có**
18. **tér**mino   ter**mi**no   termi**nó**

Part 1: 4.3   Practice with plurals

Some nouns are agudas even if they end in an 'n' or 's' (that is why they have written accent marks). Notice that in the plural they become llanas and no longer need the written mark. Sometimes the opposite is true; the singular is llana, while the plural becomes aguda and needs a mark.[6] Pronounce these words out loud and pay attention to the written marks.

1. cora**zón**   cora**zo**nes
2. lec**ción**   lec**cio**nes
3. japo**nés**   japo**ne**ses
4. ra**zón**   ra**zo**nes
5. mor**món**   mor**mo**nes
6. alma**cén**   alma**ce**nes
7. com**pás**   com**pa**ses
8. inte**rés**   inte**re**ses
9. sar**tén**   sar**te**nes
10. **vir**gen   **vír**genes
10. **jo**ven   **jó**venes
12. **or**den   **ór**denes
14. e**xa**men   e**xá**menes
14. **cri**men   **crí**menes

---

[6] Notice that if a Spanish word is llana and ends in a 's', the plural is the same as the singular (*el lunes, los lunes; la tesis, las tesis; el tórax, los tórax; la crisis, las crisis*).

Part 1: 4.4 Some interesting nouns and adjectives

Look over the following words while pronouncing them out loud. The Real Academia prefers the first pronunciation, but both are used by educated natives in different parts of the world.

1. poli**cia**ca   poli**cí**aca
2. li**bi**do   **lí**bido
3. **prís**tino   pris**ti**no
4. ce**nit**   **cé**nit
5. **fú**til   fu**til**
6. **tác**til   tac**til**
7. coc**tel**   **cóc**tel
8. car**dia**co   car**dí**aco
9. zo**dia**co   zo**dí**aco
10. pe**rí**odo   pe**rio**do
11. me**du**la   **mé**dula
12. **chó**fer   cho**fer**
13. **ví**deo   vi**de**o
14. **fút**bol   fut**bol**
15. **reu**ma   re**ú**ma
16. aus**tria**co   aus**trí**aco
17. **Sá**hara   Sa**ha**ra
18. inter**va**lo   in**tér**valo

Part 1: 4.5 Three weird plurals

A few nouns in Spanish switch stress from one syllable to another when singular or plural. These are irregular and must be memorized, but the use of the accent mark follows the regular rule for accent marks. Pronounce each pair of words focusing on the switch from one stressed syllable to another. (As far as I can tell, these are the only three nouns in Spanish that have this particular defect).

1. ca**rác**ter   carac**te**res
2. **ré**gimen   re**gí**menes
3. es**pé**cimen   espe**cí**menes

Part Two

The written accent mark

1

The rules

1. If a word ends in a vowel (*a, e, i, o, u*) or 'n' or 's' and it is not *llana*, put an accent mark over the stressed syllable.
2. If a word ends in a consonant (other than 'n' or 's') and it is not *aguda*, put an accent mark over the stressed syllable.
3. One-syllable words DO NOT have a written accent mark unless they follow the rules in the next section.
4. An accent mark will also be placed over a weak vowel ('u' or 'i') in order to break an automatic diphthong.

Words that end in a vowel (or 'n' or 's') and are not *llanas*

ha - **bló**   viv - **vió**
can - **té**   sar - **tén**
cor - **tés**   fre - ne - **sí**
mas - ti - **có**   a - **llí**
pon - **dréis**   Tim - buk - **tú**

Words that end in a consonant (not 'n' or 's') and are not *agudas*

ár - bol   **cés** - ped
chó - fer   **pós** - ter
di - **fí** - cil   **fá** - cil

Breaking natural diphthongs

ba - **úl**   **rí** - o

ha - **cí** - a   a - **ún**

Ma - **rí** - a   con - ti - **nú** - a

pa - na - de - **rí** - a   **mí** - a

dú - o   **bú** - ho

Look at the differences between the following:

rí - o	river	**rio**	he laughed
ha - **cí** - a	used to do	**ha** - cia	towards
a - **ún**	still	**aun**	including
va - **cí** - o	empty	va - **ció**	she emptied

Part 2: 1.1 Palabras llanas

No written accent marks have been included in the following words, meaning that some of them are spelled wrong. Knowing that all of them are llanas when pronounced correctly, supply the missing accent marks.

1. cancer
2. inutil
3. debil
4. mastico
5. dificil
6. creo
7. llanura
8. lapiz
9. frijoles
10. torax
11. supe
12. poster
13. apostol
14. arbol
15. nadir
16. euro
17. huesped
18. puso
19. carcel
20. caracter
21. entretuve
22. tactil
23. cenit
24. angel
25. tumulto
26. divertido
27. climax
28. tristeza
29. Ramirez
30. consciente
31. martir
32. Gonzalez

Part 2: 1.2 Palabras agudas

Knowing that all of these words are agudas when pronounced correctly, supply the missing accent marks.

1. nariz
2. señor
3. conte
4. aprendera
5. frijol
6. dieciseis
7. percibir
8. oiras
9. balonpie
10. universidad

11. devolvio
12. merced
13. frenesi
14. virtud
15. veintidos
16. distinguir
17. Uruguay
18. Alcala
19. Monterrey
20. Potosi

Part 2: 1.3 Palabras esdrújulas

Knowing that all of these words are esdrújulas when pronounced correctly, supply the missing accent marks. ¡Ojo! Las esdrújulas always have an accent mark.

1. luciernaga
2. fantastico
3. analitica
4. naufrago

5. hemisferico
6. latigo
7. cantaros
8. hidrogeno

Part 2: 1.4 Breaking diphthongs

Some of the following words contains a diphthong; in others an accent mark is needed to create hiato. Decide whether each needs an accent mark and supply it if necessary.

1. puesto
2. sueño
3. sonrie
4. ataud
5. huesos
6. cuestan
7. Sonia
8. estaria
9. creian
10. pues
11. fueron
12. dio
13. maestria
14. increible
15. pua

16. sentimientos
17. tuvieron
18. Raul
19. panaderia
20. heroina
21. farmacia
22. puedes
23. ciudad
24. cazuela
25. tia
26. vivia
27. triunfo
28. duo
29. rio
30. pais

Part 2: 1.5 Macedonia de palabras

In the following list of words, mark any missing accents. Not all words will need an accent mark.

1. besame
2. instrucciones
3. sabado
4. comprensible
5. fabula
6. furiosa
7. indudable
8. abreviacion
9. paralitico
10. facil
11. capitan
12. industria
13. martires
14. fe
15. histericos
16. miercoles
17. cafe
18. geografico

19. esplendido
20. insubstancial
21. sillon
22. fui
23. melocotones
24. nocturno
25. rehen
26. sintesis
27. volcan
28. vio
29. castillo
30. pestañas
31. dificultad
32. destruccion
33. canciones
34. santo
35. ministerio
36. facultad

2

Homophonous monosyllabic pairs

One-syllable words, when they are part of a homophone pair, are distinguished from each other by marking the one that is stressed (*tónica*) with an accent mark.

To count as a homophonous monosyllabic pair, the two words must:

1. Be just one syllable long, i.e., be monosyllabic

2. Be spelled the same, i.e., be homophonous

3. Belong to two distinct grammatical categories, i.e., nouns, verbs, pronouns, prepositions, etc.

Therefore, although the word '*ve*' is a homphone (from '*ver*' it means 'he sees' and from '*ir*' it is a command form for 'go'), since both words are verbs (in the same grammatical category), neither one carries an accent mark. Indeed they are both stressed without it.

- Federico no **ve** ninguna diferencia entre el azul y el verde.
- Anita, ¡**ve** a la tienda y cómprame un litro de gaseosa!

In contrast, the word '*se*' can have three meanings. One is a reflexive pronoun, is unstressed and does not have an accent

43

mark, and the others are both verbs (from '*ser*' it is a command for 'be' and from '*saber*' it means 'I know') and both carry a written accent.

- Carlota **se** levanta a las ocho todos los días.
- Tomasito, vamos a salir. . . ¡**sé** bueno mientras no estemos en casa!
- Ay, no **sé** la respuesta a tu pregunta.

The accent mark over these one-syllable words, does indicate that there is another similarly sounding word that does not have an accent, but the mark does not tell us what the meaning is. Accent marks, in and of themselves, never change a word's meaning, they only change its pronunciation. This change in pronunciation, however, generally changes meaning. In each of the examples above, you can hear the difference between the stressed and unstressed versions of '*ve*' and '*se*'. The stressed word can be shouted out and the sentence will still makes sense, while if you shout the unstressed word, you will hear only nonsense.

> **Never put an accent mark on a one-syllable word unless you are aware of the corresponding homophone that does not need an accent mark.**
> Oh, and memorize the list on the next page!

The list of homophonous monosyllables

This is a complete list of all of the one-syllable words that can carry an accent mark in Spanish.

	Unstressed Words		Stressed Words
el	the	él	he, him
	el anillo		*es él, es para él*
te	yourself	té	tea
	¿Cómo te llamas?		
si	if	sí	yes, himself
se	himself, herself	sé	I know, be
			¡Sé bueno!
mas	but	más	more
	Quiero, mas no puedo		*¿Quieres más?*
que	that	qué	what
	dice que viene		*¿Qué piensas?*
tu	your	tú	you
	tu libro		*¿Cómo estás tú?*
mi	my	mí	me
	mi casa		*es para mí*
de	of	dé	give
cuan	So ("tan" uso arcaico)	cuán	how
	Mira cuan largo lo tengo		*¡Cuán desgraciado soy!*
cual	which	cuál	which
	Esta carta, la cual no tiene remitente, llegó ayer		*¿Cuál es el mejor?*
quien	who	quién	who
	Hay quien dice eso		*¿Quién es esa mujer?*

One last thing

Two of the words on this list, 'si' and 'mi' have an interesting attribute: they are both names for musical notes in the diatonic scale. In English, we name these with letters A, B, C, D, E, F and G, while in Spanish they are called *do, re, mi, fa, sol, la* and *si.*[7]

The generally accepted rules for Spanish orthography do not use an accent mark on this use of *si* or *mi.* However, as you can hear in the following sentences, they are in fact prosodically stressed and should, in my opinion, carry a mark to distinguish them from their unstressed homophones. Ah, but if only I were a member of the Academy—I'd have a wee bone to pick.

Beethoven compuso una sonata en si mayor.

Quiero saber cómo tocar el acorde de mi menor
   en la guitarra.

---

[7] For the famous song in English from *The Sound of Music*, Rogers and Hammerstein (1959) changed 'sol' to 'sew' (to convenience a needle pulling thread) and 'si' to 'tea' (to allow for a drink with jam and bread).

Part 2: 2.1 One-syllable words
In each group of sentences below, the underlined one-syllable words may or may not need an accent mark. Supply it if necessary.

1. a. Melisa compró un regalo para <u>el</u>.
   b. Melisa compró un regalo para <u>el</u> hermano de su amiga.

2. a. El <u>te</u> no me gusta tanto como el café.
   b. Es importante que <u>te</u> cepilles los dientes.

3. a. Iré al cine contigo el viernes <u>si</u> tengo tiempo.
   b. Tomás siempre se reserva para <u>si</u> la mayor parte.
   c. ¿Tengo hambre? <u>Si</u>, podría comer un elefante.

4. a. No tengas miedo. <u>Se</u> valiente.
   b. En estas situaciones nunca <u>se</u> qué hacer.
   c. Ayer en la carretera <u>se</u> me pinchó una llanta.

5. a. Mi tía tiene <u>mas</u> dinero de lo que necesita.
   b. Quiero salir de vacaciones este fin de semana, <u>mas</u> tengo que trabajar.

6. a. Lo más importante es <u>que</u> digas la verdad.
   b. Me quedé con tanta vergüenza <u>que</u> no sabía <u>que</u> decir.

7. a. ¿Cómo te llamas <u>tu</u>?

   b. Son las menos diez. <u>Tu</u> avión está por salir.

8. a. El ejercicio aeróbico es muy difícil para <u>mi</u>.

   b. Recibí ayer una carta de <u>mi</u> abuela

9. a. La falta <u>de</u> dinero causa mucha tristeza.

   b. Es necesario que le <u>de</u> dinero al chófer.

10. a. Vamos a Sevilla mañana. ¿<u>Cuan</u> largo es el viaje?

    b. Mira mi vestido y <u>cuan</u> hermoso me queda.

11. a. Tienes que decidir <u>cual</u> libro te interesa más.

    b. He comprado un anillo, el <u>cual</u> voy a regalarle mañana a mi novia.

12. a. Hace poco aprendí que fue mi bisabuela <u>quien</u> robó el banco central de Londres.

    b. Quiero enterarme de <u>quien</u> está chismeando en la oficina.

3

Prosodic stress and miscellaneous accent marks

Until this point all of our examples have been about which syllable is stressed in a word. Spanish also makes a distinction between stresses at the sentence or phrasal level. If a stressed syllable needs some extra punch in comparison with other stressed syllables in the same phrase, we refer to this as a **prosodic stress** (rather than word stress). Compare the following sentences:

Natalia murió en la casa **donde** había vivido.
Dolores siempre come **cuando** llega a casa.
Salomé pensó: ¿**dónde** puse mis zapatos?
María preguntó: ¿**cuándo** vamos a comer?

It is clear that in all of these sentences the words 'donde' and 'cuando' carry penultimate stress. And since both end in vowels, they need no accent mark. However, in the last two sentences, the words need to be super-stressed so as to stand out in the phrases and make them questions. This is the essence of prosodic, or sentence-level, stress.

Interrogatives

Interrogative pronouns have a tilde over their stressed syllable to distinguish them from adverbial conjunctions. This is not an exhaustive list.

Conjunctions & Relative Pronouns	Interrogatives

Conjunctions & Relative Pronouns

que   that
Es importante que estudies.

cuando   when
Me acuesto cuando tengo sueño.

como   since/because, like, as
Como tiene gripe, está guardando cama.
Marta baila como una princesa.

donde   where
Vamos a comer donde vive mi hermano.

quien   who/that
Fue Enrique quien rompió la ventana.

porque   because
Paco ayuna porque está de régimen.

Interrogatives

qué   what
¿Qué deseas comer?

cuándo   when
¿Cuándo vas a venir?

cómo   how, what
¿Cómo te llamas?

dónde   where
¿Dónde vives?

quién   who
¿Quién escupió en el suelo?

por qué   why
¿Por qué hablas tanto?

Notice that interrogatives carry accent marks even if they are in an indirect question. Observe the following:

• Paco aprendió **cómo** son los gatos silvestres.
• No sabemos **dónde** poner el sofá.
• El profesor nos explicó el **cómo** y el **porqué**.
• No sé **quién** me escribió la carta.

Adverbs that end in "-*mente*"

In exception to the comment in Section One, that any Spanish word may have only one stressed syllable, those adverbs that end in -*mente*, actually have two stresses: one (unwritten) on the suffix -*mente*, and the original stress in the adjective from with the adverb is derived. If the adjective by itself carries a tilde, then it is maintained in the adverbial form.

If the adjective has an accent mark then the adverb with -*mente* does also.

Without marks	With marks
lenta	fácil
lentamente	fácilmente
hermosa	cómoda
hermosamente	cómodamente
espiritual	rápida
espiritualmente	rápidamente
total	crítica
totalmente	críticamente
simple	ágil
simplemente	ágilmente
alta	estúpida
altamente	estúpidamente

Miscellany

The word **aún** means '*todavía*' or 'still', while **aun** means '*incluso*' or 'even'. These words are not homonyms. The former is a two-syllable word which is aguda and needs an accent mark. The other is a one syllable word—no accent mark.

Part 2: 3.1 Interrogative stress marks

In each group of sentences below, the underlined one-syllable words may or may not need an accent mark. Supply it if necessary.[8]

1. a. Se me ha quemado la paella. ¡<u>Que</u> desastre!

   b. Federico admite <u>que</u> me quiere mucho.

   c. ¿<u>Que</u> día y a <u>que</u> hora vas a venir?

   d. Me contaron <u>que</u> mañana es tu cumpleaños.
      ¡<u>Que</u> lo pases bien!

   e. Mi hermano <u>que</u> vive en Guanajuato me dijo
      <u>que</u> su esposa tiene <u>que</u> pagar una multa.

2. a. Aprendí a bailar la chueca <u>cuando</u> vivía en
      Rancagua.

   b. Evita siempre se cae dormida <u>cuando</u> mira la
      tele.

   c. ¿<u>Cuando</u> es la fiesta de San Fermín?

   d. Quiero que me digas <u>cuando</u> saliste.

3. a. Silvia fuma <u>como</u> una chimenea.

---

[8] It is true that 'que', 'cual', 'cuan' and 'quien' were also included in the previous section. This is because these words fit into both categories: they are on the short list of one-syllable words that may carry an accent mark and they may be interrogative pronouns.

b. ¿Como se debe pagar la factura? ¿Con tarjeta de crédito o en efectivo?

c. Para desayunar, normalmente, como una magdalena con un poquito de mermelada.

d. Dijo que nos llamaría como a las dos de la tarde.

e. Explícame como has podido hacer tanto trabajo en tan poco tiempo.

4. a. Vamos a sentarnos donde nos dé la gana.

b. ¿Donde está la oficina de correos?

c. Dígame ahora mismo donde escondiste mi collar.

5. a. ¿Quien es el autor de este escándalo?

b. Necesitamos saber quien nos ayudará.

c. Es la señora Bermúdez a quien le mandé el reclamo.

6. a. Me caí en el cine porque no había luz.

b. Has fallado otra vez. Ahora tendrás que explicarme el porque.

c. ¿Por que no vienes a pasear con nosotros?

7. a. ¿Cuantos pesos necesitas para pagar la renta?

b. Margarita no me contó cuantas pastillas había tomado.

c. Vi un accidente ayer en la autopista. ¡Cuanta sangre había!

d. Mi abuela me regaló unos cuantos libros.

e. Sí, sé cuanto, pero no sé ni dónde ni cómo me van a pagar.

8. a. Jordi me entregó el informe tal y cual se lo había pedido.

b. Este es la novela de la cual te estaba hablando.

c. Dime cual es el deseo de tu corazón.

d. ¿Cuales son tus películas favoritas?

9. a. Arreglé la calefacción para que estuviéramos más cómodos.

b. ¿Me vas a contar para que me has engañado?

Part 2: 3.2 Adverbs con -*mente*

Some of these adverbs may need an accent mark. Supply it if necessary.

1. grotescamente
2. urgentemente
3. oscuramente
4. friamente
5. totalmente
6. implicitamente
7. caudalmente
8. histericamente
9. audazmente
10. completamente
11. tacitamente
12. desinteresadamente

4

Changes adopted in 2010[9]

The new orthography made several important changes to the way Spanish should be written and accent marks used. Although these rules do not have the force of law anywhere, they are in fact carefully followed by professionals in all Spanish speaking countries. This includes book, magazine and newspaper publishers, editors, and educated writers at all levels.

The general principles that seem to govern these changes are that:

1. Accent marks only mark stress in Spanish; they do not indicate or distinguish among meanings.

2. We should use accent marks only when leaving them out will result in mispronunciation due to a misplaced stress.

The result is that there are several categories of words and a few specific words that had written accents marks before 2010, but that no longer do. Although some writers still use them, due to long-standing habits or reactionary stubbornness, it is best to follow the new guidelines. They actually make a lot of sense.

---

[9] The final text of the *Ortografía de la lengua española* was approved by the complete body of directors and presidents of all of the national academies that met in Guadalajara, Mexico, on November 28, 2010.

Demonstrative pronouns

These carried a tilde over their stressed syllable to distinguish them from demonstrative adjectives. These adjectives always precede nouns, the pronouns never do. But the accent mark didn't change the words' stress and therefore did nothing but confuse students and writers. The new rule calls for no accent mark on any demonstratives at all; they simply follow the basic accent rules.

¿**Esta** camisa te gusta?
*No, debes comprar **aquélla**.
Paco, ¿has leído todos **esos** libros?
*No, **ésos** no, pero **éstos** sí los he leído.

*An asterisk before these sentences indicates that the accent mark on the bold faced word is no longer appropriate or correct.

Only the lonely

Previously he word *sólo* (with an accent mark) meant 'only' (*solamente*), while *solo* meant 'alone' (masculine singular). Notice that they are now and always have been pronounced the same.

With the 2010 rules, neither word carries an accent mark. It is true that this allows for ambiguity:

Juan trabaja solo en la cocina.
John works alone in the kitchen.
John only works in the kitchen.

This ambiguity also exists in the spoken language; the new rule reflects this and that seems proper. The accent mark served only as a sign to the reader as to what the word meant; someone hearing the sentence would be left to wonder. So, the ambiguity is not in the stress or pronunciation but rather in poor word choice. It shouldn't be fixable with an accent mark. Writers should choose better words.

O or ó

The word **o** (meaning 'or') carried an accent mark only between numerals so that it was not confused with **0** (zero). Previously we wrote:

> Quiero cinco o seis dulces.
> *Quiero 5 ó 6 dulces.

The perceived confusion was that we would misread the second sentence as 'five-hundred and six pieces of candy'. The rule now is to never put an accent mark on 'o'.

The Academy's principle is that since the mark doesn't change the stress, it is unnecessary. In addition, the stated reasoning is that since computer printed text has become so common, there is little chance that an 'o' and a '0' will be confused. I have my doubts and I believe users will continue to put an accent on the word "ó", particularly when writing by hand.

5

Exercises in context

The following exercises are actual literary texts written by native-speakers for native speakers. In each case, all accent marks have been left out. Supply the missing marks.

Part 2: 4.1 Rima LVIII[10]

¿Quieres que de ese nectar delicioso
      no te amargue la hez?
Pues aspiralo, acercalo a tus labios
      y dejalo despues.

¿Quieres que conservemos una dulce
      memoria de este amor?
Pues amemonos hoy mucho, y mañana
      digamonos ¡adios!

---

[10] Bécquer, Gustavo Adolfo. (1871). *Rimas*. Cátedra: Madrid. 1982. p. 81

Part 2: 4.2 Libro de las preguntas[11]

I

Por que los inmensos aviones
no se pasean con sus hijos?[12]

Cual es el pajaro amarillo
que llena el nido de limones?

Por que no enseñan a sacar
miel del sol a los helicopteros?

Donde dejo la luna llena
su saco nocturno de harina?

III

Dime, la rosa esta desnuda
o solo tiene ese vestido?

Por que los arboles esconden
el esplendor de sus raices?

---

[11] Neruda, Pablo. (1974). *Antología fundamental.* Pehuén: Santiago, Chile. 1988. pp. 483-484.
[12] En estos versos, el autor, Neruda, ha decidido por licencia artística eliminar los puntos de interrogación al principio de cada pregunta. Se sugiere que los estudiantes no sigan este ejemplo a menos que sean poetas incipientes.

Quien oye los remordimientos
del automovil criminal?

Hay algo mas triste en el mundo
que un tren invomil en la lluvia?

VIII

Que cosa irrita a los volcanes
que escupen fuego, frio y furia?

Por que Cristobal Colon
no pudo descubrir a España?

Cuantas preguntas tiene un gato?

Las lagrimas que no se lloran
esperan en pequeños lagos?

O seran rios invisibles
que corren hacia la tristeza?

Part 2: 4.3 Greguerías[13]

1. El craneo es la boveda alta del corazon.

2. Miercoles: dia largo por definicion.

3. A veces nos preguntamos como algun hombre malisimo puede proceder de la santa familia que ocupo el Arca, pero para comprenderlo pensamos que alguien se metio de polizon.

4. Eva fue la esposa de Adan, y ademas, su cuñada y su suegra.

5. El murcielago es un pajaro policia.

6. En los museos de reproducciones escultoricas es donde los papas oyen a los niños las cosas mas insolitas: —¡Papa, a mi no me ha salido aun la hoja!

7. No se por que la I mayuscula ha de quedarse sin su punto.

---

[13] Gómez de la Serna, Ramón. (Siglo XX). *Greguerías*. Cátedra: Madrid. 1982.

Part 2: 4.4 El padre nuestro[14]

Padre nuestro que estas en los cielos, santificado sea
tu nombre.

Venga tu reino. Hagase tu voluntad, como en el cielo,
asi tambien en la tierra.

El pan nuestro de cada dia, danoslo hoy.

Y perdonanos nuestras deudas, como tambien
nosotros perdonamos a nuestros deudores.

Y no nos metas en tentacion, mas libranos de mal.

Amen.

Part 2: 4.5 María, la boba[15]

Maria, la boba, creia en el amor. Eso la convirtio en
una leyenda viviente. A su entierro acudieron todos los
vecinos, hasta los policias y el ciego del quiosco, quien
rara vez abandonaba su negocio. La calle Republica
quedo vacia, y en señal de duelo colgaron cintas
negras en los balcones y apagaron los faroles rojos de
las casas.

---

[14] Mateo 6: 9-13. *Santa Biblia.* Versión Reina y de Valera.
[15] Allende, Isabel. (1989). *Cuentos de Eva Luna.* Sudamericana: Buenos
Aires. 1990. p. 134.

Part 2: 4.6 Elogio a la madrastra[16]

El dia que cumplio cuarenta años, doña Lucrecia encontro sobre su almohada una misiva de trazo infantil, caligrafiada con mucho cariño:

«¡Feliz cumpleaños, madrastra!

»No tengo plata para regalarte nada pero estudiare mucho, me sacare el primer puesto y ese sera mi regalo. Eres la mas buena y la mas linda y yo me sueño todas las noches contigo.

»¡Feliz cumpleaños otra vez!

»Alfonso»

---

[16] Vargas Llosa, Mario. (1988). *Elogio de la madrastra*. Emecé: Buenos Aires. 1988. p. 15.

Part 2: 4.7 El túnel[17]

Una tarde, por fin, la vi por la calle. Caminaba por la otra vereda, en forma resuelta, como quien tiene que llegar a un lugar definido a una hora definida.

La reconoci inmediatamente; podria haberla reconocido en medio de una multitud. Senti una indescriptible emocion. Pense tanto en ella, durante esos meses, imagine tantas cosas, que al verla no supe que hacer.

La verdad es que muchas veces habia pensado y planeado minuciosamente mi actitud en caso de encontrarla. Creo haber dicho que soy muy timido. . . .

La muchacha, por lo visto, solia ir a salones de pintura. En caso de encontrarla en uno, me pondria a su lado y no resultaria demasiado complicado entrar en conversacion a proposito de algunos de los cuadros expuestos.

---

[17] Sábato, Ernesto. (1948). *El túnel.* Cátedra: Madrid. 1983. p. 66.

Part 2: 4.8 La conciencia[18]

Ya no podia mas. Estaba convencida de que no podria resistir mas tiempo la presencia de aquel odioso vagabundo. Estaba decidida a terminar. Acabar de una vez, por malo que fuera, antes que soportar su tirania.

Llevaba cerca de quince dias en aquella lucha. Lo que no comprendia era la tolerancia de Antonio para con aquel hombre. No: verdaderamente, era extraño.

El vagabundo pidio hospitalidad por una noche: la noche del miercoles de ceniza, exactamente, cuando batia el viento arrastrando un polvo negruzco, arremolinado, que azotaba los vidrios de las ventanas con un crujido reseco. Luego, el viento ceso. Llego una calma extraña a la tierra, y ella penso, mientras cerraba y ajustaba los postigos:

—No me gusta esta calma.

---

[18] Matute, Ana María. (1961). *Historias de la Artámila.* Destino: Barcelona. 2000. p. 116.

Part 2: 4.9 La viuda de Montiel[19]

Cuando murio don Jose Montiel, todo el mundo se sintio vengado, menos su viuda; pero se necesitaron varias horas para que todo el mundo creyera que en verdad habia muerto. Muchos lo seguian poniendo en duda despues de ver el cadaver en camara ardiente, embutido con almohadas y sabanas de lino dentro de una caja amarilla y abombada como un melon. Estaba muy bien afeitado, vestido de blanco y con botas de charol, y tenia tan bien semblante que nunca parecio tan vivo como entonces. Era el mismo don Chepe Montiel de los domingos, oyendo misa de ocho, solo que en lugar de la fusta tenia un crucifijo entre las manos. Fue preciso que atornillaran la tapa del ataud y que lo emparedaran en el aparatoso mausoleo familiar, para que el pueblo entero se convenciera de que no se estaba haciendo el muerto.

---

[19] García Márquez, Gabriel. (1962). *Los funerales de la Mamá Grande.* Diana: México, D.F. 1986. p. 77.

Part 2: **4.10** Cantando en el pozo[20]

La casa se esta cayendo. Yo algunas veces quisiera sujetarla con las manos y todo, pero se que se esta cayendo, y nada puedo hacer.

Yo miro la casa cayendose, y pienso que alli fue donde conoci a Celestino, y donde aprendimos a jugar a la marchicha; que alli fue donde mi madre me dio el primer cintazo, y donde por primera vez me paso la mano por la cabeza. Que alli fue donde abuelo dijo una vez «Pascuas» y se rio a carcajadas, y yo me puse muy alegre cuando el dijo «Pascuas», y no se por que, me dio tanta risa y alegria, que me fui para el rincon del corredor, donde crecen las matas de tulipan, y alli, debajo del panal de avispas, me rei y me rei a mas no poder. «Pascuas» «Pascuas» «Pascuas». Y me volvi a reir a carcajadas y no sentia las avispas, que ya revoloteaban sobre mis orejas. «Pascuas» «Pascuas» «Pascuas».

Y me retorcia en el suelo, de la alegria tan grande.

---

[20] Arenas, Reinaldo. (1965). *Cantando en el pozo*. Argos Vergara: Barcelona. 1982. p. 145.

Part 2: 4.11 CRÉDITO EXTRA: Mazúrquica modérnica[21]

Me han preguntadico varias personicas[22]
si peligrosicas para las masicas
son las cancionicas agitadoricas.
¡Ay que preguntica más infantilica!
Solo un piñuflico la formularica,
pa' mis adentricos yo comentarica.

Le he contestadico yo al preguntonico:
cuando la guatica pide comidica,
pone al cristianico firme y guerrerico
por sus poroticos y sus cebollicas;
no hay regimientico que los detenguica
si tienen hambrica los popularicos. . . .

Ni los obrericos ni los paquiticos
tienen la culpita, señor fiscalico.

Lo que yo cantico es una respuestica
a una preguntica de unos graciosicos,

---

[21] Parra, Violeta. (1966). *Últimas composiciones.* RCA Víctor.
[22] Cada verso contiene dos palabras estdrújulas inventadas por la poetisa.

y mas no cantico porque no quierico:
tengo perezica en el zapatico,
en los cabellicos, en la camisica,
en los riñonicos y en el bolsillico.

6

Accent marks on a computer[23]

Please get in the habit of using the computer to type accent marks and do it as you type. This is much easier than going through a document and adding the marks afterwards. (Imagine writing in English and then going back to dot each 'i' and cross every 't' after you've finished writing!) All word processors are capable of doing proper accent marks in Spanish. Almost all printers are capable of printing them.

Below are some instructions that might help. You will only need to do this process once; your word processor will remember how you have set up these special characters.

Apple

Since the first Macintosh in 1984, every Apple computer has been capable of producing beautiful text in Spanish right "out of the box." It is also easy to use accent marks and tildes, etc., on an iPad or iPhone.

---

[23] If anyone tries to convince you to use ASCI character codes instead of the solutions described here, just smile politely and ignore them. In almost all cases, the ASCI codes are the most complicated and least intuitive way to do accent marks and special characters. They will make your life (or at least typing in Spanish) miserable.

- On any Apple computer, the grave accent mark is achieved by pressing the OPTION and 'E' keys at the same time and then, after letting go, pressing the vowel over which you want the mark.

~ The *tilde* is made by pressing the OPTION and 'N' keys, followed by the letter over which you want the tilde. In Spanish, of course, this is always an 'n'.

¿ The upside-down question mark is made by pressing OPTION and SHIFT and the '?' keys all at the same time.

¡ Likewise, the upside-down exclamation point is made by simply pressing OPTION and '1' at the same time.

.. Finally, the *crema* is produced by pressing on the option and 'u' keys, and the pressing the vowel over which you want the symbol—usually a 'u' in Spanish.

Windows

The best option is to install a Spanish keyboard in Windows. This will allow you to use accent marks in any program on the computer, including word-processing and email, but also the desktop, file names, and within graphics and gaming applications. Once installed, it is very easy to switch back and forth between English and Spanish.

After you install a Spanish keyboard the letters on your actual keyboard (the hardware) will not necessarily indicate what letter or symbol will be typed: your computer thinks you have an actual Spanish keyboard. The layout on a Spanish keyboard is slightly different; that is, some symbols are in different places than they are on the English (American) keyboard. This layout is represented here. You can either memorize where the new keys are or use a marker or label-maker to indentify where the Spanish symbols are.

ª	|	"	·	$	%	&	/	(	)	=	?	¿	
º	1	2	3	4	5	6	7	8	9	0	'	¡	Backspace

	Q	W	E	R	T	Y	U	I	O	P	^	*	Ç
Tab	q	w	e	r	t	y	u	i	o	p	`	+	ç

	A	S	D	F	G	H	J	K	L	Ñ	"		
Caps	a	s	d	f	g	h	j	k	l	ñ	'	Enter

Shift	Z	X	C	V	B	N	M	;	:	_		
	z	x	c	v	b	n	m	,	.	-	Shift

Spanish Keyboard Layout

To switch in Windows between the Spanish keyboard and English keyboard, simply press the ALT and SHIFT keys at the same time. A small icon in the lower right corner of the task bar will change from ES to EN and vice versa. Wondrously, in Microsoft Word this will also enable the Spanish spelling checker. (But don't rely on the spelling checker to catch your accent mark problems; it misses a lot of them).

To type an accent mark on a Spanish keyboard, hit the apostrophe followed by the vowel over which you want the mark. The "ñ" is the colon key; "Ñ" is a capital colon. Question marks ("¿" and "?") are the "+" and "_" symbols respectively. The upside down exclamation is the "=" key.

Installing the keyboard

The details vary depending on which version of Windows you are using, but in broad strokes:

- Click first on "Start" and then open the "Control Panel."
- Once there double-click on "Regional and Language Options" (If you are in an older version of windows, click on "Keyboard" in the "Control Panel").
- Now select the "Languages" tab (or "Keyboards and Languages") at the top of the new window and then click on "Details" or "Change keyboards."
- Under "Installed services" you can see any keyboards that you have already installed.
- To add a Spanish keyboard, click on "ADD".
- There is a long list of Spanish spell-checkers available. Any one will do, but I suggest "Spanish (International Sort)" which will alphabetize lists the correct (modern) way. The program will automatically select the "Spanish Variation" keyboard.
- Click "OK" to exit the control panel.

Now (perhaps after you restart your computer) you will see a small square near your system tray (the lower right row of icons on the task bar at the bottom of your screen in Windows). Clicking on this little square (or pressing the CTRL and SHIFT keys at the same time) will give you the option of toggling back and forth between any keyboards you have installed. Again, EN is for English and ES is for Spanish (español).

Good luck!

Microsoft Word in Office

If you only want to do accent marks in MS Word, the program is shipped set up and ready to go. The default keystrokes for accented characters are as follows:

´   Press the CTRL and the "'" (apostrophe) keys at the same time then let go. Now press the vowel over which you wish to place the accent mark.

~   Press three keys, the CTRL, SHIFT and '~' at the same time and then let go. Now type an 'n' or 'N'.

¿   Press four keys and hold them all down at once: ALT, CTRL, SHIFT and '?'.

¡   Similarly, press four keys: ALT, CTRL, SHIFT and '!'.

¨   To make the crema, press CTRL, SHIFT and ':', release and then press 'u'.

Answers to exercises

1.1 Counting syllables

1. _2_ mesa
2. _2_ lento
3. _4_ fatalidad
4. _2_ triste
5. _6_ lastimosamente
6. _3_ contento

7. _3_ mostrador
8. _5_ adulterado
9. _2_ falta
10. _4_ pontífice
11. _5_ hipotético
12. _5_ contabilidad

Part 1: 1.2 Stressed syllables

1. humo[ro]sa
2. [jue]gan
3. [sín]tomas
4. can[tad]
5. resta u[ran]te
6. [sá]bana

7. fri[jol]
8. fri[jol]es
9. [ár]boles
10. asis[ten]te
11. mostra[dor]
12. ligera[men]te

Part 1: 2.1 Finding Diphthongs

1. genera[ción]
2. m[ue]stra
3. maestra
4. [hia]to
5. caz[ue]a
6. teatral

7. espontáneo
8. lic[ue]facción
9. aéreo
10. concupiscen[cia]
11. saeta
12. [eu]ropeo

Part 1: 2.2 Finding 'hitao'

1. generación
2. muestra
3. m[a-e]stra
4. hiato
5. cazuela
6. [e-a]tral

7. espontán[e-o]
8. licuefacción
9. [a-é][e-o]
10. concupiscencia
11. s[a-e]ta
12. europ[e-o]

Part 1: 2.3 Counting syllables

1. _4_ generación
2. _2_ muestra
3. _3_ maestra
4. _2_ hiato
5. _3_ cazuela
6. _3_ teatral

7. _5_ espontáneo
8. _4_ licuefacción
9. _4_ aéreo
10. _5_ concupiscencia
11. _3_ saeta
12. _4_ europeo

Part 1: 3.1 Counting syllables in one-syllable words

1. _1_ las
2. _1_ pues
3. _1_ diez
4. _1_ guion
5. _1_ aun
6. _1_ buen

7. _1_ ya
8. _1_ buey
9. _1_ fui
10. _1_ dios
11. _1_ vio
12. _1_ cien

Part 1: 4.1 Which syllable is stressed?

	LLANA	AGUDA	ESDRÚJULA	SOBRES.
1. **pa**tio	■	❑	❑	❑
2. na**riz**	❑	■	❑	❑
3. sim**pá**tico	❑	❑	■	❑
4. **sá**bana	❑	❑	■	❑
5. contes**tó**	❑	■	❑	❑
6. con**tes**to	■	❑	❑	❑
7. ac**ción**	❑	■	❑	❑
8. ac**cio**nes	■	❑	❑	❑
9. mur**cié**lago	❑	❑	■	❑
10. hi**pér**baton	❑	❑	■	❑
11. ca**du**co	■	❑	❑	❑
12. frene**sí**	❑	■	❑	❑
13. man**dí**bula	❑	❑	■	❑
14. intere**san**te	■	❑	❑	❑
15. **quí**tamelo	❑	❑	❑	■

PART TWO

Part 2: 1.1 Palabras llanas

1. **cáncer**	17. **huésped**
2. **inútil**	18. puso
3. **débil**	19. **cárcel**
4. mastico	20. **carácter**
5. **difícil**	21. entretuve
6. creo	22. **táctil**
7. llanura	23. **cénit**
8. **lápiz**	24. **ángel**
9. frijoles	25. tumulto
10. **tórax**	26. divertido
11. supe	27. **clímax**
12. **póster**	28. tristeza
13. **apóstol**	29. **Ramírez**
14. **árbol**	30. consciente
15. **nádir**	31. **mártir**
16. euro	32. **González**

Part 2: 1.2 Palabras agudas

1. nariz	11. **devolvió**
2. señor	12. merced
3. **conté**	13. **frenesí**
4. **aprenderé**	14. virtud
5. frijol	15. **veintidós**
6. **dieciséis**	16. distinguir
7. percibir	17. Uruguay
8. **oirás**	18. **Alcalá**
9. **balonpié**	19. Monterrey
10. universidad	20. **Potosí**

Part 2: 1.3 Palabras esdrújulas

1. lu**ciér**naga	5. hemis**fé**rico
2. fan**tás**tico	6. **lá**tigo
3. ana**lí**tica	7. **cán**taros
4. **náu**frago	8. hi**dró**geno

81

Part 2: 1.4 Breaking diphthongs

1. puesto
2. sueño
3. **sonríe**
4. **ataúd**
5. huesos
6. cuestan
7. Sonia
8. **estaría**
9. **creían**
10. pues
11. fueron
12. dio
13. **maestría**
14. **increíble**
15. **púa**

16. sentimientos
17. tuvieron
18. **Raúl**
19. **panadería**
20. **heroína**
21. farmacia
22. puedes
23. ciudad
24. cazuela
25. **tía**
26. **vivía**
27. triunfo
28. **dúo**
29. rio or **río**
30. **país**

Part 2: 1.5 Macedonia de palabras

1. **bésame**
2. instrucciones
3. **sábado**
4. comprensible
5. **fábula**
6. furiosa
7. indudable
8. **abreviación**
9. **paralítico**
10. **fácil**
11. **capitán**
12. industria
13. **mártires**
14. fe
15. **histéricos**
16. **miércoles**
17. **café**
18. **geográfico**

19. **espléndido**
20. insubstancial
21. **sillón**
22. fui
23. melocotones
24. nocturno
25. **rehén**
26. **síntesis**
27. **volcán**
28. vio
29. castillo
30. pestañas
31. dificultad
32. **destrucción**
33. canciones
34. santo
35. ministerio
36. facultad

1. a. . . . un regalo para **él**.
   b. . . . un regalo para el hermano. . . .
2. a. El **té** no me gusta. . . .
   b. Es importante que te cepilles. . . .
3. a. Iré . . . si tengo tiempo.
   b. . . . se reserva para **sí** la mayor parte.
   c. . . . **Sí**, podría comer un elefante.
4. a. . . . **Sé** valiente.
   b. . . . nunca **sé** qué hacer.
   c. . . . en la carretera se me pinchó una llanta.
5. a. Mi tía tiene **más** dinero . . . .
   b. Quiero salir . . . mas tengo que trabajar.
6. a. Lo más importante es que digas la verdad.
   b. . . . tanta vergüenza que no sabía **qué** decir.
7. a. ¿Cómo te llamas **tú**?
   b. . . . Tu avión está por salir.
8. a. . . . es muy difícil para **mí**.
   b. . . . carta de mi abuela
9. a. La falta de dinero . . . .
   b. Es necesario que le **dé** dinero . . . .
10. a. . . . ¿**Cuán** largo es el viaje?
    b. Mira mi vestido y cuan hermoso me queda.
11. a. . . . decidir **cuál** libro te interesa más.
    b. He comprado un anillo, el cual voy a . . . .
12. a. . . . fue mi bisabuela quien robó el banco . . . .
    b. . . . enterarme de **quién** está chismeando . . . .

1. a. . . . ¡**Qué** desastre!
   b. . . . admite <u>que</u> me quiere mucho.
   c. ¿**Qué** día y a **qué** hora vas a venir?
   d. Me contaron <u>que</u> mañana es tu cumpleaños.
      ¡<u>Que</u> lo pases bien!
   e. Mi hermano <u>que</u> vive en Guanajuato me dijo
      <u>que</u> su esposa tiene <u>que</u> pagar una multa.
2. a. Aprendí a bailar . . . <u>cuando</u> vivía . . . .
   b. . . . se cae dormida <u>cuando</u> mira la tele.
   c. ¿**Cuándo** es la fiesta . . . ?
   d. Quiero que me digas **cuándo** saliste.
3. a. . . . fuma <u>como</u> una chimenea.
   b. ¿**Cómo** se debe pagar . . . ?
   c. Para desayunar. . . <u>como</u> una magdalena. . . .
   d. . . . nos llamaría <u>como</u> a las dos . . . .
   e. Explícame **cómo** has podido . . . .
4. a. Vamos a sentarnos <u>donde</u> nos dé la gana.
   b. ¿**Dónde** está la oficina . . . ?
   c. Dígame . . . **dónde** escondiste mi collar.
5. a. ¿**Quién** es el autor de este escándalo?
   b. Necesitamos saber **quién** nos ayudará.
   c. Es la señora Bermúdez a <u>quien</u> le mandé . . . .
6. a. Me caí . . . <u>porque</u> no había luz.
   b. . . . tendrás que explicarme el **porqué**.
   c. ¿**Por qué** no vienes a pasear . . . ?

7. a. ¿**Cuántos** pesos necesitas . . . ?

   b. . . . no me contó **cuántas** pastillas . . . .

   c. . . . ¡**Cuánta** sangre había!

   d. . . . me regaló unos <u>cuantos</u> libros.

   e. . . . sé **cuánto**, pero no sé . . . .

8. a. . . . me entregó el informe tal y <u>cual</u> se lo había
      pedido.

   b. . . . es la novela de la <u>cual</u> te estaba hablando.

   c. Dime **cuál** es el deseo . . . .

   d. ¿**Cuáles** son tus películas favoritas?

9. a. Arreglé . . . <u>para que</u> estuviéramos . . . .

   b. ¿ . . . contar **para qué** me has engañado?

Part 2: 3.2 Adverbs con *-mente*

1. grotescamente		7. caudalmente	
2. urgentemente		8. **histéricamente**	
3. oscuramente		9. audazmente	
4. **fríamente**		10. completamente	
5. totalmente		11. **tácitamente**	
6. **implícitamente**		12. desinteresadamente	

Part 2: 4.1 Rima LVIII

¿Quieres que de ese **néctar** delicioso
    no te amargue la hez?
Pues **aspíralo, acércalo** a tus labios
    y **déjalo después**.

¿Quieres que conservemos una dulce
    memoria de este amor?
Pues **amémonos** hoy mucho, y mañana
    digámonos ¡adiós!

Part 2: 4.2 Libro de las preguntas

I

Por **qué** los inmensos aviones
no se pasean con sus hijos?

Cuál es el **pájaro** amarillo
que llena el nido de limones?

Por **qué** no enseñan a sacar
miel del sol a los **helicópteros**?

Dónde dejó la luna llena
su saco nocturno de harina?

III

Dime, la rosa **está** desnuda
o solo tiene ese vestido?

Por **qué** los **árboles** esconden
el esplendor de sus **raíces**?

Quién oye los remordimientos
del **automóvil** criminal?

Hay algo **más** triste en el mundo
que un tren **inmóvil** en la lluvia?

VIII

Qué cosa irrita a los volcanes
que escupen fuego, **frío** y furia?

Por **qué Cristóbal Colón**
no pudo descubrir a España?

Cuántas preguntas tiene un gato?

Las **lágrimas** que no se lloran
esperan en pequeños lagos?

O **serán ríos** invisibles
que corren hacia la tristeza?

Part 2: 4.3 Greguerías

1. El **cráneo** es la **bóveda** alta del **corazón**.
2. **Miércoles**: **día** largo por **definición**.
3. A veces nos preguntamos como **algún** hombre **malísimo** puede proceder de la santa familia que **ocupó** el Arca, pero para comprenderlo pensamos que alguien se **metió** de **polizón**.
4. Eva fue la esposa de **Adán**, y **además**, su cuñada y su suegra.
5. El **murciélago** es un **pájaro policía**.
6. En los museos de reproducciones **escultóricas** es donde los **papás** oyen a los niños las cosas **más insólitas**: —¡**Papá**, a **mí** no me ha salido **aún** la hoja!
7. No **sé** por **qué** la I **mayúscula** ha de quedarse sin su punto.

Part 2: 4.4 El padre nuestro

Padre nuestro que **estás** en los cielos, santificado sea tu nombre.

Venga tu reino. **Hágase** tu voluntad, como en el cielo, **así también** en la tierra.

El pan nuestro de cada **día**, **dánoslo** hoy.

Y **perdónanos** nuestras deudas, como **también** nosotros perdonamos a nuestros deudores.

Y no nos metas en **tentación**, mas **líbranos** de mal.
   Amén.

Part 2: 4.5 María, la boba

María, la boba, **creía** en el amor. Eso la **convirtió** en una leyenda viviente. A su entierro acudieron todos los vecinos, hasta los **policías** y el ciego del quiosco, quien rara vez abandonaba su negocio. La calle **República quedó vacía**, y en señal de duelo colgaron cintas negras en los balcones y apagaron los faroles rojos de las casas.

Part 2: 4.6 Elogio a la madrastra

El **día** que **cumplió** cuarenta años, doña Lucrecia **encontró** sobre su almohada una misiva de trazo infantil, caligrafiada con mucho cariño:
«¡Feliz cumpleaños, madrastra!
»No tengo plata para regalarte nada pero **estudiaré** mucho, me **sacaré** el primer puesto y ese **será** mi regalo. Eres la **más** buena y la **más** linda y yo me sueño todas las noches contigo.
»¡Feliz cumpleaños otra vez!
»Alfonso»

Part 2: 4.7 El túnel

Una tarde, por fin, la vi por la calle. Caminaba por la otra vereda, en forma resuelta, como quien tiene que llegar a un lugar definido a una hora definida.

La **reconocí** inmediatamente; **podría** haberla reconocido en medio de una multitud. **Sentí** una indescriptible **emoción**. **Pensé** tanto en ella, durante esos meses, **imaginé** tantas cosas, que al verla no supe **qué** hacer.

La verdad es que muchas veces **había** pensado y planeado minuciosamente mi actitud en caso de encontrarla. Creo haber dicho que soy muy **tímido**. . . .

La muchacha, por lo visto, **solía** ir a salones de pintura. En caso de encontrarla en uno, me **pondría** a su lado y no **resultaría** demasiado complicado entrar en **conversación** a **propósito** de algunos de los cuadros expuestos.

Part 2: 4.8 La conciencia

Ya no **podía más**. Estaba convencida de que no **podría** resistir **más** tiempo la presencia de aquel odioso vagabundo. Estaba decidida a terminar. Acabar de una vez, por malo que fuera, antes que soportar su **tiranía**.

Llevaba cerca de quince **días** en aquella lucha. Lo que no **comprendía** era la tolerancia de Antonio para con aquel hombre. No: verdaderamente, era extraño.

El vagabundo **pidió** hospitalidad por una noche: la

noche del **miércoles** de ceniza, exactamente, cuando **batía** el viento arrastrando un polvo negruzco, arremolinado, que azotaba los vidrios de las ventanas con un crujido reseco. Luego, el viento **cesó**. **Llegó** una calma extraña a la tierra, y ella **pensó**, mientras cerraba y ajustaba los postigos:

—No me gusta esta calma.

Part 2: 4.9 La viuda de Montiel

Cuando **murió** don **José** Montiel, todo el mundo se **sintió** vengado, menos su viuda; pero se necesitaron varias horas para que todo el mundo creyera que en verdad **había** muerto. Muchos lo **seguían** poniendo en duda **después** de ver el **cadáver** en **cámara** ardiente, embutido con almohadas y **sábanas** de lino dentro de una caja amarilla y abombada como un **melón**. Estaba muy bien afeitado, vestido de blanco y con botas de charol, y **tenía** tan bien semblante que nunca **pareció** tan vivo como entonces. Era el mismo don Chepe Montiel de los domingos, oyendo misa de ocho, solo que en lugar de la fusta **tenía** un crucifijo entre las manos. Fue preciso que atornillaran la tapa del **ataúd** y que lo emparedaran en el aparatoso mausoleo familiar, para que el pueblo entero se convenciera de que no se estaba haciendo el muerto.

La casa se **está** cayendo. Yo algunas veces quisiera sujetarla con las manos y todo, pero **sé** que se **está** cayendo, y nada puedo hacer.

Yo miro la casa **cayéndose**, y pienso que **allí** fue donde **conocí** a Celestino, y donde aprendimos a jugar a la marchicha; que **allí** fue donde mi madre me dio el primer cintazo, y donde por primera vez me **pasó** la mano por la cabeza. Que **allí** fue donde abuelo dijo una vez «Pascuas» y se rio a carcajadas, y yo me puse muy alegre cuando **él** dijo «Pascuas», y no **sé** por **qué**, me dio tanta risa y **alegría**, que me fui para el **rincón** del corredor, donde crecen las matas de **tulipán**, y **allí**, debajo del panal de avispas, me **reí** y me **reí** a **más** no poder. «Pascuas» «Pascuas» «Pascuas». Y me **volví** a **reír** a carcajadas y no **sentía** las avispas, que ya revoloteaban sobre mis orejas. «Pascuas» «Pascuas» «Pascuas».

Y me **retorcía** en el suelo, de la **alegría** tan grande.

Me han **preguntádico** varias **persónicas**
si **peligrósicas** para las **másicas**
son las **canciónicas agitadóricas**.
¡Ay que **pregúntica más infantílica**!
Solo un **piñúflico** la **formulárica**,
pa' mis **adéntricos** yo **comentárica**.

Le he **contestádico** yo al **preguntónico**:
cuando la **guática** pide **comídica**,
pone al **cristiánico** firme y **guerrérico**
por sus **poróticos** y sus **cebóllicas**;
no hay **regimiéntico** que los **deténguica**
si tienen **hámbrica** los **populáricos**. . . .

Ni los **obréricos** ni los **paquíticos**
tienen la **cúlpita**, señor **fiscálico**.

Lo que yo **cántico** es una **respuéstica**
a una **pregúntica** de unos **graciósicos**,
y **más** no **cántico** porque no **quiérico**:
tengo **perézica** en el **zapático**,
en los **cabéllicos**, en la **camísica**,
en los **riñónicos** y en el **bolsíllico**.

A select historical bibliography

On spelling

1741. *Ortografía de la lengua española.* Real Academia Española. Madrid.

1959. *Nuevas normas de prosodia y ortografía.* Real Academia Española. Madrid.

1999. *Ortografía de la lengua española.* Real Academia Española. Espasa Calpe: Madrid. (162 pages)

2010. *Ortografía de la lengua española.* Real Academia Española/Asociación de Academias de la Lengua Española. Espasa Libros (España) y Editorial Planeta (México): México, D.F. (743 pages)

On grammar

1492. Antonio de Nebrija. *Gramática de la lengua castellana.* Salamanca.

1771. *Nueva gramática de la lengua española.* Real Academia Española. Madrid.

1931. *Gramática de la lengua española.* Real Academia Española. Madrid.

1973. *Esbozo de una nueva gramática de la lengua española.* Real Academia Española. Espasa-Calpe: Madrid. (589 pages).

2010. *Nueva gramática de la lengua española:* Real Academia Española/Asociación de Academias de la Lengua Española. Espasa Libros (España) y Editorial Planeta (México): México, D.F. (3,800 pages)

National Academies
of the Spanish Language

1713	Real Academia Española.
1871	Academia Colombiana de la Lengua
1874	Academia Ecuatoriana de la Lengua
1875	Academia Mexicana
1876	Academia Salvadoreña de la Lengua
1883	Academia Venezolana de la Lengua
1885	Academia Chilena de la Lengua
1887	Academia Peruana de la Lengua
1887	Academia Guatemalteca de la Lengua
1923	Academia Costarricense de la Lengua
1924	Academia Filipina de la Lengua Española
1926	Academia Panameña de la Lengua
1926	Academia Cubana de la Lengua
1927	Academia Paraguaya de la Lengua Española
1927	Academia Boliviana de la Lengua
1927	Academia Dominicana de la Lengua
1928	Academia Nicaragüense de la Lengua
1931	Academia Argentina de la Lengua
1943	Academia Nacional de Letras de Uruguay
1949	Academia Hondureña de la Lengua
1955	Academia Puertorriqueña de la Lengua Española
1973	Academia Norteamericana de la Lengua Española

A VISUAL GUIDE TO ACCENT MARKS

Read the book first and this will make perfect sense.

Does a word need an accent mark?

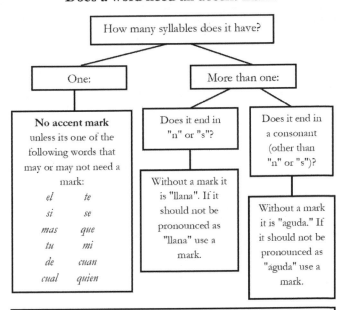

How many syllables does it have?

One:

No accent mark
unless its one of the
following words that
may or may not need a
mark:

el	*te*
si	*se*
mas	*que*
tu	*mi*
de	*cuan*
cual	*quien*

More than one:

Does it end in
"n" or "s"?

Without a mark it
is "llana". If it
should not be
pronounced as
"llana" use a
mark.

Does it end in
a consonant
(other than
"n" or "s")?

Without a mark
it is "aguda." If
it should not be
pronounced as
"aguda" use a
mark.

In addition:

• Use an accent mark to break a natural diphthong: *ía, ío, aú*, etc.

• Use an accent mark on interrogative pronouns: ¿*cuál, qué, quién*? etc.

• Words that are converted into adverbs with -*mente* maintain an accent
mark if they have one.

Made in the USA
Middletown, DE
06 July 2022